IN FOCUS

ROCKS AND FOSSILS

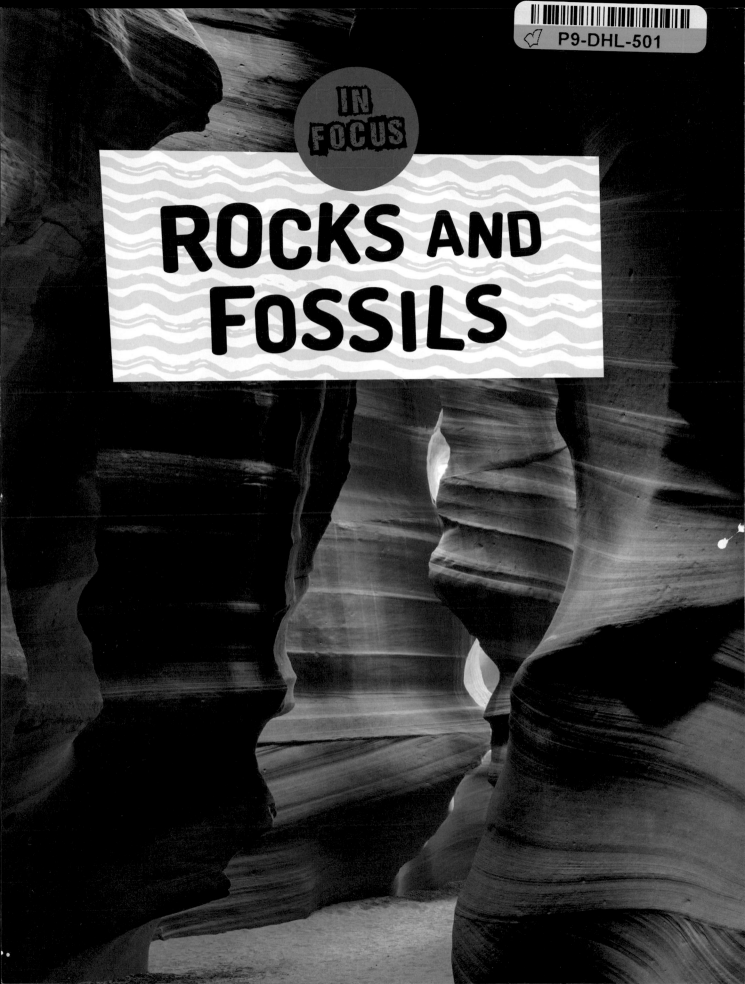

KINGFISHER
LONDON & NEW YORK

Copyright © Macmillan Publishers International Ltd 2018
Published in the United States by Kingfisher,
175 Fifth Ave., New York, NY 10010
Kingfisher is an imprint of Macmillan Children's Books, London
All rights reserved.

Distributed in the U.S. and Canada by Macmillan,
175 Fifth Ave., New York, NY 10010

Library of Congress Cataloging-in-Publication data has been applied for.

Series editor: Hayley Down
Designer: Jeni Child

ISBN (PB): 978-0-7534-7427-3
ISBN (HB): 978-0-7534-7426-6

Kingfisher books are available for special promotions
and premiums. For details contact: Special Markets
Department, Macmillan, 175 Fifth Ave.,
New York, NY 10010.

For more information, please visit
www.kingfisherbooks.com

Printed in China

9 8 7 6 5 4 3 2 1

1TR/0418/WKT/UG/128GSM

Picture credits
The Publisher would like to thank the following for permission to reproduce their material. Every care has been taken
to trace copyright holders.
Top = t; Bottom = b; Center = c; Left = l; Right = r
Front cover: iStock/alxpin; Back cover: iStock/Vershinin-M; Cover flap: iStock/Natalia-flurno; Pages 1 iStock/adogslifephoto; 3 Alamy/
Peter Cripps; 4–5 iStock/weisschr; 4, 27t, 61 NASA/JPL-Caltech/UCLA/MPS/DLR/IDA/PSI; 4 iStock/Theanthrope; 5c iStock/Studio-
Annika; 6 iStock/espiegle; 7t iStock/guenterguni; 7c iStock/Vadim Svirin; 7b Shutterstock/BGSMith; 8–9 iStock/simonbradfield;
10 iStock/kavram; 11t Alamy/Johan Swanepoel; 11b iStock/Justinreznick; 12t Shutterstock/Hugh O'Connor; 12b iStock/Beboy_ltd;
12t iStock/lucky-photographer; 14–15 Getty/David Lyons; 15 iStock/sara_winter; 16–17 iStock/MikeMcFarlane; 16bl iStock/draco-zlat;
16br Getty/David Lyons; 17bl Alamy/Mike Robinson; 17br Alamy/Matthijs Wetterauw; 18–19 iStock/Jamalrani; 20 Alamy/Alan Keith
Beastall; 21t iStock/cinoby; 21c iStock/Mlenny; 21b iStock/Sanderstock; 22–23 iStock/Grafissimo; 23 Alamy/PjrStudio; 24 iStock/
imagepotpro; 24 (1) Shutterstock/usagi2013; 24 (2) Shutterstock/Mongkolchon Akesin; 25 (3) Shutterstock/Zelenskaya; 25 (4) iStock/
Tree4Two; 25 (5) Shutterstock/ruttanapol comfoo; 25 (6) Shutterstock/vvoe; 25 (7) iStock/t:krzystofdek; 25 (8) iStock/Difydave;
25 (9) iStock/Pi-Lens; 25 (10) iStock/joecicak; 26–27 iStock/bjdlzx; 27b NASA; 28–29 iStock/dogausufdokdok; 30 NHM; 31t iStock/
phantit; 31c iStock/Dovapi; 31b iStock/Alteryourreality; 32t iStock/La_Corivo; 32bl iStock/Baldomir; 32br Shutterstock/PNSJ88;
33t iStock/justin_zoll; 33c iStock/PK6289; 33bl iStock/Sergdid; 33br iStock/Stellar-Serbia; 34–35 Getty/Carsten Peter/Speleoresearch
& Films; 36 Alamy/Ian Mansfield; 37t Shutterstock/Kalabi Yau; 37c Shutterstock/Sean Pavone; 37b iStock/FrankvandenBergh;
38 iStock/mariusz_prusaczyk; 39t Alamy/Greenshoots Communications; 39b iStock/Dazman; 40–41 iStock/sdlgzps; 42 (1) Getty/
SpencerPlatt; 42 (2) Shutterstock/Potapov Alexander; 42 (3) iStock/Reimphoto; 42 (4) iStock/murboy; 43 (5) Alamy/Corbin17;
43 (6) iStock/miljko; 43 (7) iStock/Reimphoto; 43 (8) iStock/Gam1983; 43 (9) iStock/Fred_Pinheiro; 43 (10) iStock/Kerrick;
44–45 Alamy/Corbin17; 46 Alamy/Tony French; 47t iStock/CoreyFord; 47c iStock/Zheka-Boss; 47b Shutterstock/MarcelClemens;
48 iStock/milehightraveler; 49t NHM; 49b Creative Commons; 50–51 Alamy/Jeff J Daly; 52 (1) iStock/Aunt_Spray; 53 (2) Alamy/
Nobumichi Tamura/Stocktrek Images; 53 (3) Creative Commons; 53 (4) Alamy/Bertrand Gardel; 53 (5) Alamy/herraez; 53 (6) Alamy/
Ingo Schulz; 53 (7) iStock/estt; 53 (8) iStock/loonger; 53 (9) iStock/Mark Kostich; 53 (10) iStock/NHM, London; 54–55 SPL/Sinclair
Stammers; 56 iStock/jzabloski; 57t Alamy/Chronicle; 57b iStock/jarino47; 58tl Alamy/NHM; 58tr iStock/leonello; 58b & 59tl Alamy/
NHM; 59tr Alamy/Philip Brownlow/Stocktrek Images; 59b Alamy/Pictorial Press; 60 iStock/BruceBlock; 62 iStock/LucynaKoch;
63 iStock/tpnagasima.

ROCKS AND FOSSILS

BY **CHRIS OXLADE**

KINGFISHER
NEW YORK

CONTENTS

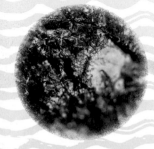

WELCOME TO THE WORLD OF ROCKS

Wherever you are on Earth's surface, there are rocks under your feet. You'll always find them if you dig down far enough! These rocks make up Earth's rocky outer layer—the **crust**. Earth's surface seems like a solid place to live, but rocks are changing all the time. Just think about molten rock spewing from **volcanoes**, and rocks crumbling into the ocean at the **coast**. These changes have been happening for billions of years. Fossils are part of rocks. They are the rocky remains of animals and plants that lived long ago.

Kjeragbolten, Norway

6

INSIDE YOU'LL FIND . . .

. . . tough rocks

Learn about the different types of **ROCK**, and how rocks are made, destroyed, and transformed in an incredible process called the **rock cycle**.

. . . magical minerals

Discover all you need to know about the stuff that rocks are made from, and see some stunning **MINERAL CRYSTALS**, including diamonds, sapphires, and other precious gemstones.

. . . fantastic fossils

Wonder at the incredible **FOSSILS** found in rock. They tell us what life on Earth was like hundreds of millions of years ago.

AMAZING ROCKS

You can see the rocks that make up Earth's crust in mountains, at coasts, and in canyons, where they are **EXPOSED**.

EARTH'S ROCKY SURFACE

Let's begin our exploration of rocks by discovering some key facts about Earth's rocky outer layer: the crust.

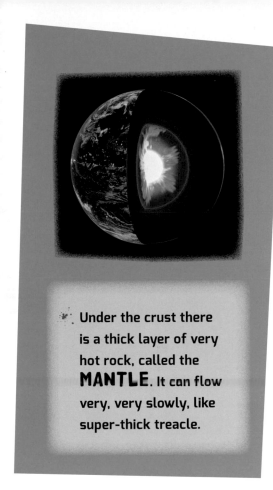

Under the crust there is a thick layer of very hot rock, called the **MANTLE**. It can flow very, very slowly, like super-thick treacle.

* Earth's crust is made up of giant pieces, called **TECTONIC PLATES**. They move around, but only as fast as your fingernails grow.

* Earth's **CRUST** is up to 43.5 mi (70 km) thick under the land, but just 3 mi (5 km) thick under the **ocean floor**.

* Where tectonic plates crash into each other, towering **MOUNTAIN RANGES** are formed as the plates are pushed up against each other.

* Rocks from the crust are useful **MATERIALS**. Beautiful marble is a rock that is often used for ornaments, tiles, and worktops.

* Volcanoes erupt when hot, molten rock, called **MAGMA**, escapes from the mantle, through the crust, and onto Earth's surface. Volcanoes are found where the edges of tectonic plates meet.

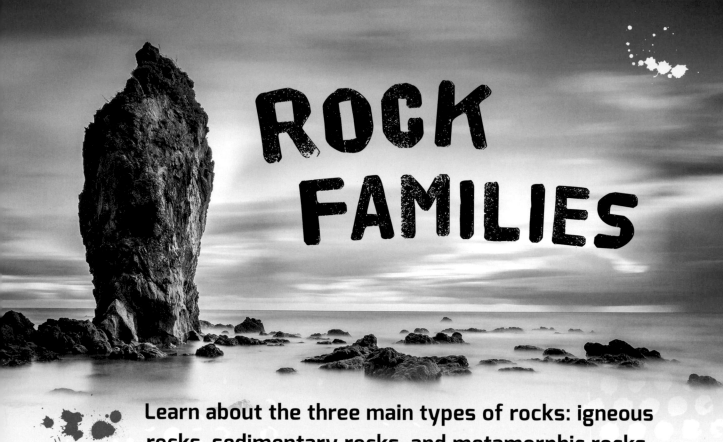

ROCK FAMILIES

Learn about the three main types of rocks: igneous rocks, sedimentary rocks, and metamorphic rocks.

FIERY IGNEOUS ROCKS

Most rock on Earth is igneous rock. Igneous rocks are made from fiery magma from the mantle. When a volcano erupts, the magma that flows onto Earth's surface is called **lava**. Flowing lava cools and turns to solid rock. Some volcanoes blast magma into the air as ash.

The ash falls to the ground and builds into thick layers that cool into new rock. Magma often rises into Earth's crust, but gets trapped underground, where it cools slowly to form new igneous rock.

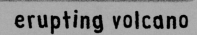

erupting volcano

LAYERED SEDIMENTARY ROCKS

Sticky mud, fine silt, and soft sand are all made up of tiny bits of rock. They are called **sediment**. They are found in riverbeds, on the ocean floor, and in deserts.

When layers of sediment get buried under more layers of sediment, they very slowly turn into solid rock. This kind of rock is called sedimentary rock.

Monument Valley, Utah

TRANSFORMED METAMORPHIC ROCKS

It's burning hot deep down in Earth's crust! The pressure on rocks is immense too, so the rocks are squeezed extremely tightly and often folded. This heat and pressure can change igneous rocks and

sedimentary rocks into a whole new type of rock: metamorphic rocks. These rocks are usually found down in the crust under huge **mountain ranges**, such as the Himalayas.

Himalayas, Nepal

FIERY ROCKS

Your questions about igneous rocks answered!

How much lava comes from a volcano?

The biggest volcanic eruption we know of started about 66 million years ago, in India. The lava kept flowing for millions of years. It flooded the surrounding landscape with layers of new rock. All the lava would have filled a cube 50 mi (80 km) high. The rocky landscape created by this eruption is now called the Deccan Traps.

How fast does lava flow?

Some lava is thick and gooey, and creeps along at just a few feet every hour. Other lava is thin and runny. It can reach speeds of 37 mph (60 kph)—you couldn't escape it, even on a bicycle! This runny lava can flow a long way before it cools down. An old lava flow in Queensland, Australia, is 99 mi (160 km) long!

erupting volcano

What are volcanoes made of?

Volcanoes build up into hills and mountains. They are made from lava that turns to rock, ash, and small chunks of rock, called cinders. Volcanoes with gently sloping sides are made mostly from solidified lava. They are called shield volcanoes. Steep-sided volcanoes are made from layers of cooled lava and ash that have fallen to the ground. They are called composite volcanoes.

composite volcano

Do volcanoes erupt under the ocean?

Yes! There are hundreds of volcanoes under the ocean. When lava pours into the water, it cools very quickly and forms rounded lumps that look like pillows, so it is called "pillow lava." The tips of giant, undersea volcanoes form volcanic islands, such as the islands of Hawaii in the Pacific Ocean.

PECULIAR ROCKS

WATERFALLS AND WHITE ROCKS

These pools and waterfalls have formed at Pamukkale in Turkey. The white walls are made from a rock called travertine. Hot water flows up from underground springs that contain **minerals**. The rock builds up from the minerals as the water trickles along. **Stalactites** and **stalagmites** form in the same way.

Pamukkale, Turkey

WHERE A GIANT WALKED

There are about 40,000 columns of rock at the Giant's Causeway on the coast of County Antrim in Northern Ireland. The rock is basalt that erupted from a volcano about 50 million years ago. The rock cracked as it cooled and shrank, forming hexagonal columns. Legend says that a giant called Finn McCool made the Giant's Causeway.

Giant's Causeway, Ireland

Find out about some of the world's weird and wonderful rocks!

FLOATING ROCKS

Can you believe that there is rock that floats on water? This rock does. It's called pumice, and it's often found around volcanoes. Chunks of pumice form when lava full of bubbles of gas is blasted from a volcano, like red-hot foam. The rock quickly cools in the air and becomes solid, trapping bubbles that make the rock very lightweight.

pumice seen from ship

BUCKLED ROCKS

These layers of sedimentary rock are folded into zigzags. After they were formed, huge forces underground pushed and pulled on them. The rocks folded in the same way as a rug if you push it from both ends. These folding forces are made by Earth's tectonic plates moving around and by magma pushing up from the mantle.

folded rock

CLOSE UP

ROCKY WAVES

Rocks can be beautiful! Layer upon layer of sedimentary rocks, some thick, some thin, create these spectacular and colorful swirls. This sedimentary rock is called sandstone. It's made up of billions of sand particles fused together. Wind and water have worn away the rock to leave deep canyons surrounded by steep cliffs that reveal the rocky layers.

Sand dunes

These cliffs are found in the Vermilion Cliffs National Monument. The sandstone layers were made hundreds of millions of years ago from sand dunes blown by the wind.

DESTROYING ROCKS

The pebbles and grains of sand you find on a beach are bits of rock. They were made when the weather, the wind, and flowing water broke up large rock into tiny bits. Old rocks are always being destroyed in this way, and new rocks are made from their sediment. This process is called the rock cycle.

ROCKING FACT

On mountains, it is often warm in the day and freezing at night. Water trickles into cracks in the rocks during the day and freezes to ice at night. The ice widens the cracks, weakening the rock. When the effects of the weather slowly break solid rocks into pieces, we call it **WEATHERING**.

weathered rocks in Derbyshire, England

seawater eroding rocks

Bits of rock are carried away from mountains or coasts by water flowing down streams or rivers, and by waves crashing against the shore. This is called **EROSION**. Strong winds erode rocks by blowing away loose bits from their surface.

These spiky rocks are made of limestone. The limestone is being slowly eaten away by rainwater, which is slightly acidic, a bit like lemon juice. The rock gradually **DISSOLVES**, creating deep canyons and underground caves.

limestone karst

river sediments

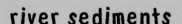
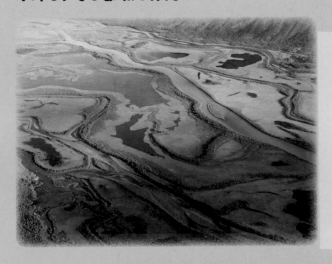

Millions of bits of **SEDIMENT** are washed down rivers. Sediment gets dumped at the mouth of rivers to form an area of land called a delta. When sediment gets buried under more sediment, it turns into sedimentary rock.

USEFUL ROCKS

Your questions about how we use rocks answered!

What can we make from rocks?

Sculptors shape rocks with saws and chisels to make statues, sculptures, and ornaments. These ancient Moai sculptures on Easter Island are made mostly from tuff and basalt. Worktops and tiles are made from rocks such as marble and slate. You can even use hot volcanic rocks to cook your food!

Moai, Easter Island, Chile

How can we use rocks?

Tough, heavy rock boulders are placed on our coastlines to protect them against erosion from giant waves. Crushed rock is used for hard-wearing road surfaces, and gravel is an ingredient in **concrete**.

Why do we mine for coal?

Coal is a sedimentary rock that people have **mined** and burned for fuel for thousands of years. Coal is a type of fossil fuel, which means it is made from dead plants that rotted and transformed into rock over millions of years.

Are there any rock artifacts?

Many thousands of years ago people learned to chip away at rocks, such as flint, to make sharp tools, such as these arrowheads, along with ax heads and knives.

flint arrowheads

TOP 10 COMMON ROCKS

Keep an eye out for these rocks that you can often see in the countryside and in buildings.

1 Basalt

Basalt is the most common rock of all! It's an igneous rock that's made when runny lava cools quickly. It's fine-grained, which means the grains of the minerals it's made of are too small to see without looking through a magnifying glass.

Gneiss

That's pronounced "nice." If you see swirls of black and white like this, it's probably gneiss—a metamorphic rock formed deep under mountain ranges.

Granite

An igneous rock with big **crystals**, granite forms when underground magma cools slowly. You can see its grains, making it coarse-grained.

Sandstone

When sand in riverbeds, on beaches, or in deserts gets buried, it turns to sandstone. Sandstone is a sedimentary rock found all over the world.

Marble

You might see marble in a kitchen or bathroom. Marble is a metamorphic rock made from limestone. It has attractive swirls and patterns of different colors.

Pegmatite

You can recognize pegmatite from its large crystals, which can be many inches long. It's an igneous rock, formed when magma cools very slowly underground.

Shelly limestone

No surprise that this sedimentary rock is full of the shells of sea creatures. Shelly limestone is made from the shells of dead sea creatures that sink to the seabed.

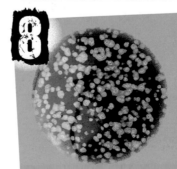

Obsidian

Glassy obsidian is often carved into beautiful ornaments. It's also called volcanic glass, and it's formed when lava cools very quickly.

Conglomerate

Take a mixture of rocky lumps or pebbles, sand, or mud, turn it to rock, and you have conglomerate. The rocky lumps and pebbles can be any kind of rock.

Slate

Slate is mudstone turned into a metamorphic rock by huge pressure deep underground. Slate splits easily into thin sheets.

Which rock is your number one?

These spectacular shooting stars in the night sky are tiny bits of rock from space hurtling into Earth's atmosphere and burning up. Each tiny bit of rock is called a **METEOR**.

SPACE ROCKS

There's a lot of rock in space— on the Moon, on other planets, and hurtling through the Asteroid Belt.

About **100 TONS** of space rock hit Earth's atmosphere every day. Nearly all of this rock burns up harmlessly.

Between 1969 and 1972, the astronauts of the Apollo missions collected 60 st (382 kg) of **MOON ROCK** from the lunar surface and brought it back to Earth. Moon rock is very similar to rock found on Earth.

An **ASTEROID** is a lump of rock drifting around in space. Asteroids look like giant potatoes! Most are in the Asteroid Belt, between Mars and Jupiter. This asteroid is called Vesta. It's 326 mi (525 km) across.

The other planets made of rock in our **Solar System** are Mercury, Venus, and Mars. Along with Earth, these are known as the **ROCKY PLANETS**.

A lump of space rock that hits Earth's surface is a **METEORITE**. One meteorite smashed into the ground in Australia in 1969. It weighed more than 15 st (100 kg).

MARS is known as the "Red Planet." The rocks on its surface contain lots of iron that has gone rusty, giving Mars its red color.

MIGHTY
MINERALS

MEET THE MINERALS

All rocks are made of minerals. A few rocks are made from just one, but most are made from two or more mixed together. Altogether there are hundreds and hundreds of minerals. Some form shapes called crystals and come in beautiful colors and patterns. These are called precious or semi-precious gemstones.

ROCKING A FACT

In this lump of **ZINC ORE**, you can see the different minerals; they are the small pieces with different colors. The main minerals in this rock are calcite (pink), willemite (green), zincite (blue), and franklinite (black).

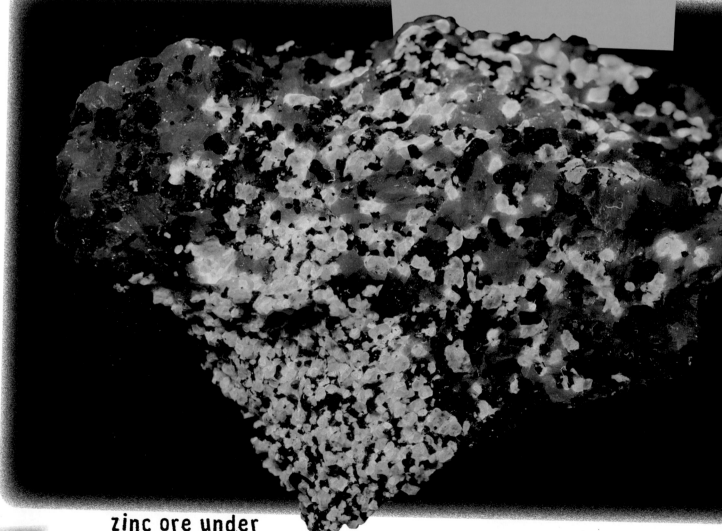

zinc ore under fluorescent light

calcite columns

These **STALACTITES** (the spikes pointing down) and **STALAGMITES** (the spikes sticking up) are made of a mineral called calcite. The mineral is left behind when water containing it drips from the cave roof.

real or fake?

ROCKING a FACT

Some people mistake this rock for gold, which is why it's nicknamed **"FOOL'S GOLD."** It's actually a mineral called pyrite, made from iron and sulfur.

dry up!

ROCKING a FACT

The water in some lakes tastes very, very salty. It's full of minerals such as **HALITE**, which is the same stuff that we put in our food. When the lake water dries up, it leaves a crusty white salt behind.

INCREDIBLE CRYSTALS

CRYSTAL CUBES

Minerals naturally grow into crystals of different shapes. Each different shape has a name. These shiny gray crystals are made of a mineral called galena, which contains lead and sulfur. Galena crystals grow in perfect cubes, which are known as cubic crystals. Halite (that's everyday table salt) also has cubic crystals that you can see by looking at salt through a magnifying glass.

galena

LONG AND LEAN

Sulfur is a yellow mineral. Its crystals are often shaped a little like cubes that are flattened and then stretched in one direction, a bit like a matchbox. This shape of crystal is called orthorhombic (pronounced "or-tho-rom-bic"). Sulfur crystals often grow around the vents of volcanoes and around hot springs, where boiling water rises from underground.

sulfur

When minerals have space to grow, they often form beautiful shapes with flat sides and straight edges, called crystals.

SIX SIDES

These crystals are made of the mineral quartz. They are shaped like rods with six sides and pointy ends—a bit like a six-sided pencil sharpened at one end. A shape with six sides is called a hexagon, so crystals of this shape are known as hexagonal crystals.

quartz

SHINY SHAPES

Some minerals don't form neat crystals with flat sides and straight edges. But they do grow in shapes of their own. This mineral is hematite. The rounded, lumpy shape of the mineral is called reniform. It's sometimes called kidney ore because it's shaped like a kidney, and because it's an ore of iron (which means we get iron from it).

hematite

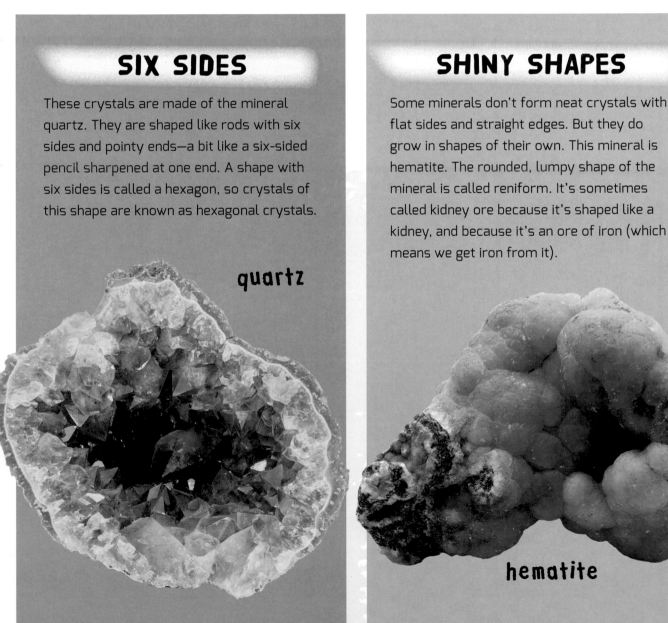

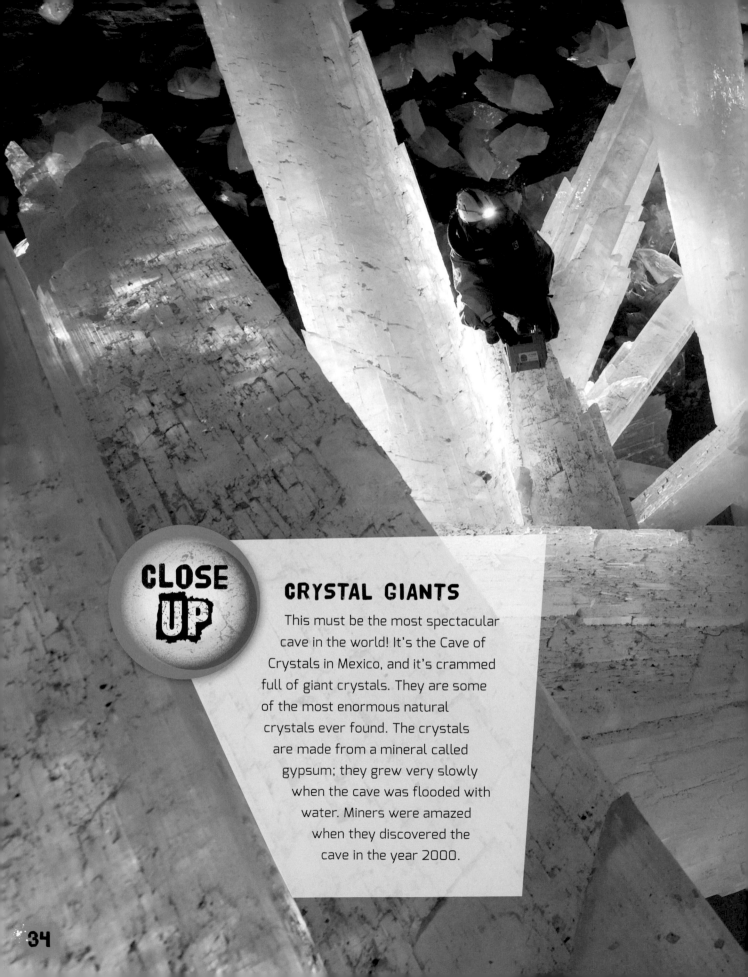

CLOSE UP

CRYSTAL GIANTS

This must be the most spectacular cave in the world! It's the Cave of Crystals in Mexico, and it's crammed full of giant crystals. They are some of the most enormous natural crystals ever found. The crystals are made from a mineral called gypsum; they grew very slowly when the cave was flooded with water. Miners were amazed when they discovered the cave in the year 2000.

More about the cave

- The longest crystal measures 40 ft (12 m) long, 13 ft (4 m) round, and weighs over 50 tons.
- It took 500,000 years for the crystals to grow.
- The cave is 980 ft (300 m) below Earth's surface.

PRACTICAL AND PRECIOUS MINERALS

Do you know what jewelry, **fertilizers**, and medicines have in common? The answer is minerals—the minerals found in rocks! The jewels in jewelry are pieces of colorful or sparkly minerals, fertilizers contain minerals called phosphates and nitrates, and some medicines contain a mineral called kaolin. Minerals are really useful raw materials.

ROCKING FACT

A priceless royal **CROWN** is studded with spectacular jewels. The jewels are called precious gemstones. They are crystals of minerals, such as diamonds and sapphires. They are valuable because they are rare.

tough minerals

Some minerals are super tough, which makes them good for jobs such as sawing and grinding. This stone-cutting disc has hundreds of tiny **DIAMONDS** stuck to it.

essential minerals

CONCRETE is vital for builders. They use loads of it. Cement is like the glue that sticks together the gravel and sand in concrete. The main ingredient in cement is calcium oxide, and calcium oxide is made from the mineral calcium carbonate.

edible minerals

Halite is the mineral name for salt. It's also called **ROCK SALT**. In some places, it forms layers underground. Here it is stored at a salt mine, where it is dug from the ground.

Hundreds of millions of tons of **IRON ORE** are dug out of the ground every year to produce all the iron and steel we need. Massive diggers and trucks take the ore from the ground. This image shows the view from above.

GET THE METALS OUT

We use metals to make all sorts of objects, from gold jewelry to steel ships. All metals come from minerals.

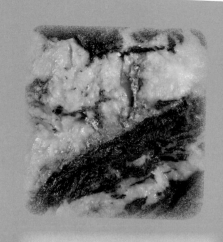

- The minerals we get metals from are called **ORE MINERALS**. For example, we get copper from a mineral called bornite and lead from the mineral galena.

- The minerals have to be processed to remove the metals. First the minerals are crushed. Then they are melted to release the metals. This process is called **SMELTING**.

- Aluminum is strong but lightweight, and it's good for building planes as well as saucepans. We get aluminum from a rock called **BAUXITE**, which is a mixture of different minerals.

- **GOLD** and **COPPER** were the first metals to be discovered by people. They were easy to see inside their minerals and could be extracted before smelting was invented.

- **EXPLOSIONS** are sometimes used in mining to break big chunks of rock away from cliffs, mountains, or caves.

IN THE FURNACE

It's not easy to take the iron out of iron ore. The ore must be heated in a huge container called a blast furnace until it reaches 2912°F (1600°C). The largest blast furnaces today can produce about 80,000 tons of iron per week.

More about smelting

People have been smelting rocks to obtain the metals inside them for thousands of years. The oldest blast furnaces were built in China around 1 CE.

PRECIOUS GEMS

Which are the most beautiful and precious gemstones?

1

Diamond.

The hardest of all minerals, diamond is difficult to scratch, so it stays sparkly for years! Diamonds are found in rough shapes and carefully cut for jewelry. The largest ever found weighed more than a pound!

2

Sapphire

Sapphire comes in blues, yellows, greens, and pinks. It is a type of corundum, which is the second-hardest mineral.

3

Ruby

Ruby is a form of the mineral corundum. An element called chromium gives it a blood-red color.

4

Emerald.

This gem is made from a mineral called beryl. Another gemstone, aquamarine, is also a form of beryl.

7 Garnet

Red, orange, and yellow garnets are valuable, but green is rarest. The word "garnet" comes from the Latin for "pomegranate."

8 Jade

This green semi-precious gem is often carved into ornaments. It's made from minerals called jadeite or nephrite.

9 Topaz

Topaz is a popular gem because it's quite common in rocks. Giant topaz crystals weigh up to 220 lbs (100 kg)!

5 Opal

Opal is carved and polished to make gems. There are white opal, milky opal and black opal, which is the most precious form.

10 Turquoise

This blue-green-colored gemstone gives its name to the color turquoise. It was one of the first gemstones people discovered.

6 Amethyst

Violet or purple forms of the mineral quartz are called amethyst. The jewelers of Ancient Egypt put amethyst in their necklaces and rings.

Which gem is your number one?

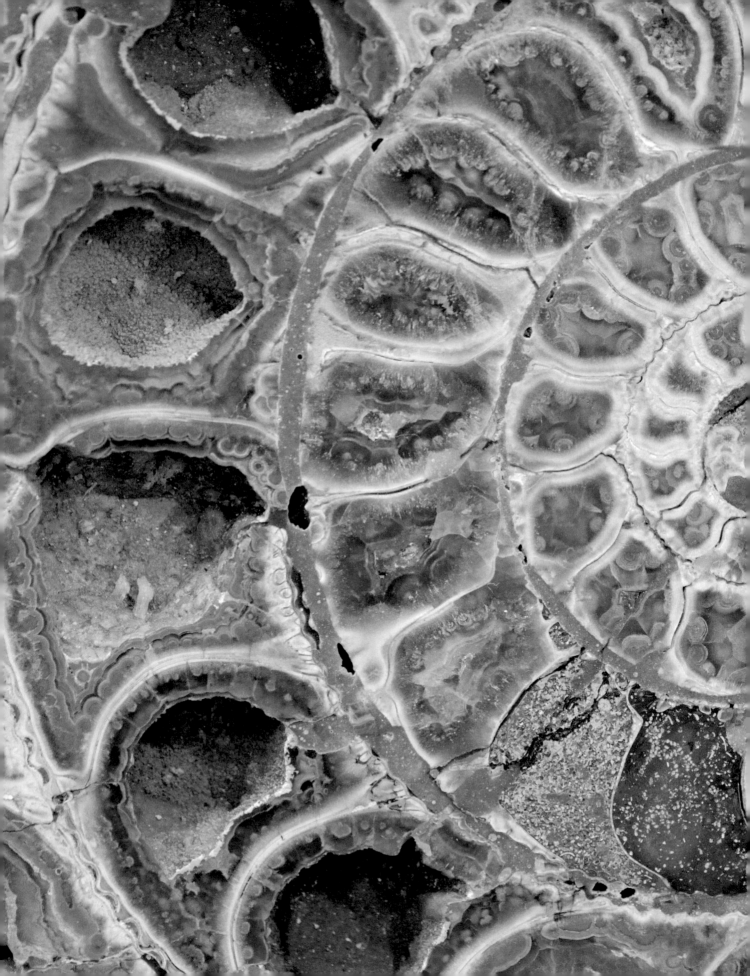

FANTASTIC
FOSSILS

UNEARTH THE FOSSILS

Who isn't fascinated by **dinosaurs**? These incredible creatures lived millions of years ago. How do we know about them? The answer is simple: fossils. Fossils are the remains of plants and animals that have turned to rock. They tell us about life on Earth in the distant past.

Meet Sophie the **STEGOSAURUS!** Sophie's fossilized bones were discovered in 2003 in Wyoming. Her skeleton was almost complete. Sophie was a young Stegosaurus when she died about 150 million years ago. She stood about 10 ft (3 m) high, nearly 20 ft (6 m) long, and weighed about 1.5 tons.

Sophie the Stegosaurus

visualizing the past

Scientists can figure out the **AGE** of the rocks they find fossils in. This tells them how long ago the animals or plants that formed the fossil lived. This picture gives an idea of Earth in **Jurassic** times, more than 65 million years ago.

fossil layers

Most fossils are found in layers of sedimentary rocks. The remains of the animals or plants were **TRAPPED** as the rocks formed. In layers of rock, the younger fossils are found in higher layers than the older fossils.

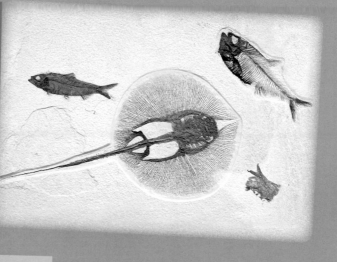

fossil rocks

Some rocks are made of nothing but fossils. These could be fossils of shells, as in this **SHELLY LIMESTONE**, or the fossils of the skeletons of tiny marine animals. The shells or skeletons sink to the ocean floor, where they become fossilized.

TRACE FOSSILS
are fossils of things
such as animal
footprints, poop, and
nests. They tell us more
about how the animals
lived and moved.

48

FOSSIL
FORMATION

Most fossils are made when animal or plant remains are trapped in sediments and become part of sedimentary rocks.

* This fossil is so tiny you can only see it through a microscope. It's called a **MICROFOSSIL**.

* Fossils most often form when animals and plants get **BURIED** quickly in wet silt or clay before they rot away. This happens in rivers and on the ocean floor.

* The **OLDEST** fossils ever found are thought to be around 4 billion years old. The fossils are of tiny microorganisms, called **bacteria**, which could have been the first living things on Earth.

* As you are reading this book, **NEW FOSSILS** are being made in sedimentary rocks. They might be found in millions of years' time.

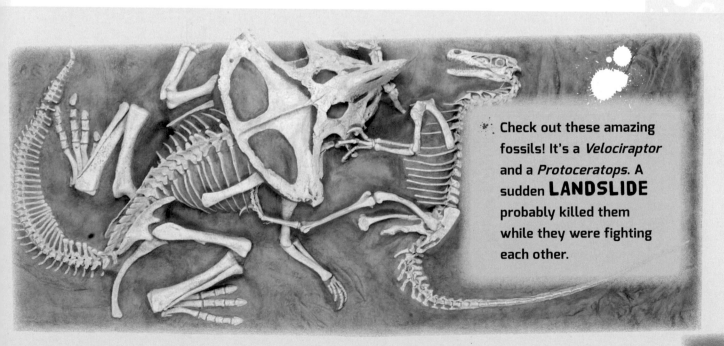

* Check out these amazing fossils! It's a *Velociraptor* and a *Protoceratops*. A sudden **LANDSLIDE** probably killed them while they were fighting each other.

CLOSE UP

TRAPPED IN SAP

Millions of years ago this unlucky insect was trapped in gooey tree sap. The sap was fossilized and turned to a mineral called amber, with the insect still inside. In 2015, archaeologists in Myanmar discovered a complete dinosaur tail fossilized in amber—it still had flesh, bones, and even feathers!

More about amber

Amber has been prized for its beauty since 10,200 BCE, being used for jewelry and folk medicines. The oldest amber fossil ever found is a staggering 320 million years old!

TOP 10

FOSSILS THROUGH TIME

Here are some fossils that have helped us to understand when different kinds of animals started living on Earth.

1 Trilobites

These bug-like sea creatures lived on Earth for a very, very long time. The oldest trilobite fossils are about 520 million years old. Trilobites became extinct (died out completely) about 250 million years ago.

2 First fish

Fish began to appear in lakes, rivers, and seas from about 500 million years ago. They were the first creatures to have skeletons,

7 Giant ammonites

Ammonites were sea creatures like squid, with long tentacles. They lived in the seas when dinosaurs lived on the land.

3 Onto the land

The first animals that climbed out of the sea onto the land were amphibians (modern-day frogs and newts are amphibians).

8 Dragonflies

Here is a fossil of one of the largest-ever flying insects. Meganeura was a huge dragonfly up to 30 in (70 cm) wide.

4 First land plants

Around 400 million years ago, there were no plants on Earth. Fossils tell us that by 360 million years ago, plants, such as this fern, had grown.

9 Smilodon

In the La Brea tar pits of California, scientists found the largest ever collection of sabertooth bones.

5 Dinosaurs

Imagine finding this extraordinary fossil! It's the skull of a huge plant-eating dinosaur, called a Triceratops. The bony frill around its neck protected it from attack.

10 Humans

This human skull was found in Morocco and is the oldest skull ever found. Experts think that it's about 31,500 years old.

6 Flying reptiles

This is the fossil of a flying reptile, called a Pterosaur. The biggest had a wingspan of 40 ft (12 m), but some were sparrow-sized.

Which fossil is your number one?

CLOSE UP

FOSSILIZED FLIPPERS

Here's a fantastic fossil of a creature called a *Plesiosaur*. The fossil shows that the *Plesiosaur* had a long neck and tail, a small head, and four big flippers. It was a reptile that lived at the same time as the dinosaurs, but it lived in the ocean. It probably used its neck to lift its head above the water to breathe, and also to reach down into the water to catch fish.

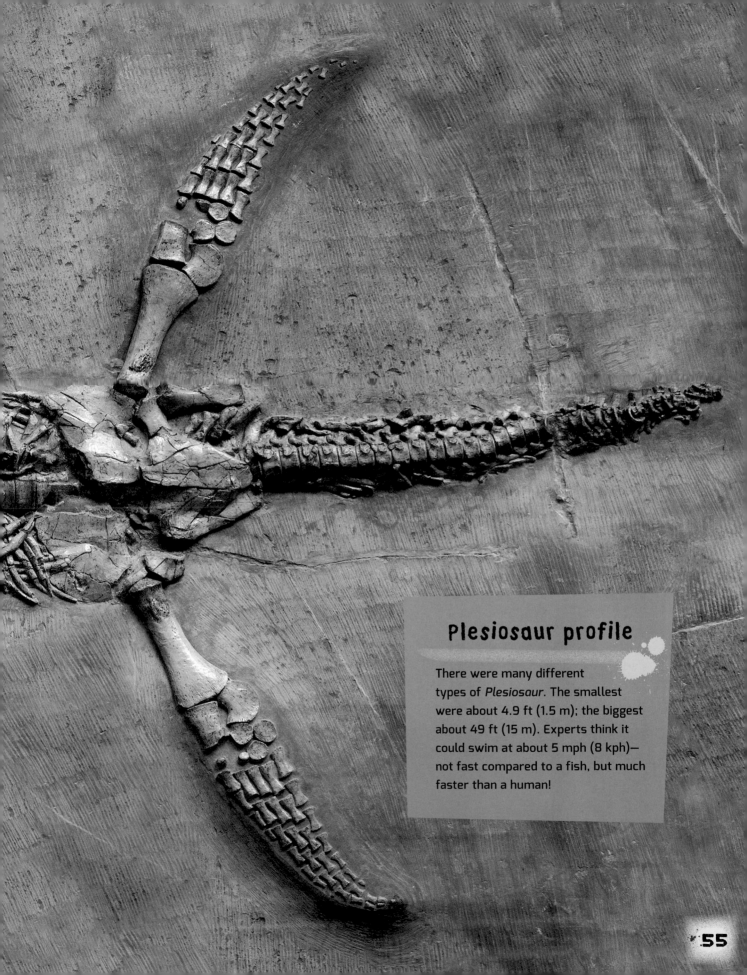

Plesiosaur profile

There were many different types of *Plesiosaur*. The smallest were about 4.9 ft (1.5 m); the biggest about 49 ft (15 m). Experts think it could swim at about 5 mph (8 kph)—not fast compared to a fish, but much faster than a human!

What big **TEETH** you have! This skull belongs to a complete T. rex fossil that was discovered in South Dakota and called Sue. Sue lived about 66 million years ago.

FABULOUS FOSSILS

Here are some of the most interesting fossils ever found.

A famous **DINOSAUR BIRD FOSSIL** that was half dinosaur, half bird was so well preserved that even its delicate feathers showed up. The fossil proved that birds are descended from dinosaurs.

A piece of **FOSSILIZED POOP** is called a coprolite. Some people polish coprolites and turn them into ornaments or jewelry—yuck!

Many perfectly preserved **MAMMOTH** fossils have been dug from frozen ground. In 1806, scientist Michael Friedrich Adams recovered a mammoth fossil and had it rebuilt in a Russian museum. It was one of the first attempts at reconstructing the skeleton of an extinct animal.

One **MEGA TOOTH** fossil, 8 in (20 cm) long, came from the jaw of a giant shark, called Megalodon. The shark was up to 26 ft (18 m) long, making it the largest shark that ever lived!

There are many **ANCIENT** fossils from a type of tree that still grows today. Fan-shaped, gingko-leaf fossils prove the tree **species** is 200 million years old.

READY TO HATCH This nest of eggs was laid millions of years ago by a dinosaur. But they never hatched.

IGUANODON

FOSSIL FINDERS

GIDEON MANTELL

Born: 1790, England
Died: 1852
Nationality: British
Important finds: *Iguanodon* tooth, dinosaur era

Gideon Mantell was a doctor in Lewes, England. His hobby was fossil hunting. He dug up dozens of fossils from the landscape around his home and even wrote books about them. In 1822 he found a fossilized tooth. It was nothing like any tooth he had found before—it was enormous! Mantell realized that it must belong to a giant plant-eating lizard, like an iguana, but much bigger. Bigger, in fact, than any land animal alive today. He gave the animal the name *Iguanodon*, meaning "iguana tooth." Mantell wrote a scientific essay called *The Age of Reptiles* that said there was an age in the past when giant reptiles roamed Earth. Many other scientists of the time thought Mantell was wrong, but he was proved to be right as more dinosaur fossils were discovered.

Gideon Mantell

People have been unearthing fossils for thousands of years. These important fossil hunters helped us to understand the secrets that fossils hold.

MARY ANNING

Born: 1799, England
Died: 1847
Nationality: British
Important finds: *Plesiosaur*, *Ichthyosaur*, and *Pterosaur*

with flippers. Nobody had ever seen one before. This discovery made her famous. She went on to find the complete skeletons of a *Plesiosaur* and a *Pterosaur*.

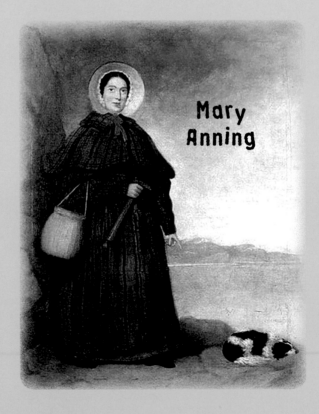

Mary Anning

Mary Anning came from a poor family that lived in the English seaside town of Lyme Regis. As a child, she walked on the beach with her father and brothers and sisters. The rocks in the cliffs at Lyme Regis were formed under the sea about 200 million years ago. They are full of fossils. Anning found lots of fossils on her walks. She sold them to visitors to the town to make money for her family. Anning didn't go to school, but she taught herself to read and write, and studied geology and biology so she could learn about the fossils. In 1811, Anning found a skeleton of an *Ichthyosaur*, like a huge fish

THE RIOTOUS ROCKS QUIZ

Are you an expert on all things rocky? Test your knowledge by completing this quiz! When you've answered all of the questions, turn to page 63 to find your score.

 1 Which type of rock is made from fiery magma that turned solid as it became cool?
a) Icarus
b) Igneous
c) Ingenious

 2 What is the name for the rocky remains of dead animals or plants?
a) Fossils
b) Metals
c) Minerals

 3 What is the name for the layer of Earth that is under the crust and consists of hot molten rock?
a) Cantle
b) Mantle
c) Pantle

 4 Which rock can float on water?
a) Basalt
b) Marble
c) Pumice

 5 What do we call the pieces of Earth's crust that move around at the same speed that your fingernails grow?
a) Tectonic plates
b) Television plates
c) Teronic plates

 6 Which type of rock is made up of layers of fine silt and sand that have become solid over time?
a) Igneous
b) Metamorphic
c) Sedimentary

 7 Which rock is full of shells of dead sea creatures?
a) Shelly granite
b) Shelly limestone
c) Shelly marble

 8 Which of these rocks is metamorphic?
a) Basalt
b) Pegmatite
c) Slate

9 What is the name for a piece of space rock that hits Earth's surface?
a) Asteroid
b) Meteor
c) Meteorite

Which planet is known as the "Red Planet?"
a) Mars
b) Uranus
c) Venus

 What is the name for a type of crystal that is lumpy and irregular in shape?
a) Cubic
b) Reniform
c) Uniform

 Which mineral are the crystals in the Cave of Crystals made of?
a) Gypsum
b) Halite
c) Zincite

 What is the name for the process of melting minerals in order to extract the metals they contain?
a) Melting
b) Smelting
c) Welting

 Which is the world's hardest mineral?
a) Diamond
b) Jade
c) Opal

 What is the name for a fossil that is so tiny that it can only be seen through a microscope?
a) Macrofossil
b) Microfossil
c) Minifossil

 What is the name for a piece of fossilized poop?
a) Amber
b) Coprolite
c) Marble

 What is a triloblte?
a) A bug-like sea creature
b) A cubic mineral
c) A metamorphic rock

 What is the name for the biggest shark ever to have existed?
a) Great white shark
b) Megalodon
c) Tiger shark

 Which scientist wrote a book called _The Age of Reptiles_?
a) Charles Darwin
b) Gideon Mantell
c) Mary Anning

GLOSSARY

bacteria
A large, varied group of very tiny, single-celled living things. Bacteria live in soil, water, plants, and animals.

canyon
A large valley with very steep sides and usually a river flowing through it.

coast
An area of land next to an ocean.

concrete
A strong building material made by mixing together cement, gravel, sand, and water.

crust
The outer layer of Earth, or any other planet, which is made of rocky pieces, called tectonic plates.

crystal
A kind of rock that is usually see-through and sometimes colorful.

dinosaurs
Prehistoric reptiles, such as Stegosaurus. Dinosaurs once ruled our planet, but died out 65 million years ago.

erupt
To suddenly break or burst. A volcano erupts when molten rock breaks through Earth's crust.

fertilizer
A substance that is added to soil to help plants grow. Fertilizers contain important nutrients and minerals

Jurassic
Describes a period of time approximately 180 million to 135 million years ago. Early birds and plants lived during this time.

lava
Hot, molten rock that erupts onto the surface of a planet and starts to flow.

mine
To dig out coal, metal, and other natural materials from the surface of a planet or other body in space.

species
A group of living things that share similar features and can breed together to produce fertile young.

stalactite
A rock formation that looks like a cone and points downward from the roof of a cave.

stalagmite
A rock formation that looks like a cone and points upward from the floor of a cave.

volcano
An opening in Earth's crust through which melted rock, ash, and gases are forced out

mineral
A natural solid that forms crystals. Minerals do not come from animals or plants but living things need them to stay alive.

mountain range
A long row or chain of high peaks, on land or underwater.

rock cycle
The process of rock formation, where rocks are worn away by erosion or weathering, the sediment builds up, and a new rock is formed from the sediment.

sediment
Fine silt or sand at the bottom of a body of water.

skeleton
The strong supporting framework of a living thing. Fish, amphibians, reptiles, birds, and mammals have an inner skeleton of bones.

solar system
A group of objects including a star and anything in orbit around it, including planets, comets, and moons.

QUIZ ANSWERS: 1 = b, 2 = a, 3 = b, 4 = c, 5 = a, 6 = c, 7 = b, 8 = c, 9 = c, 10 = a, 11 = b, 12 = a, 13 = b, 14 = a, 15 = b, 16 = b, 17 = a, 18 = b, 19 = b.

INDEX